This journal belongs to:

CONGRATULATIONS!
The most important thing you've done is
purchase this journal. It is a start. You
still have more to do, but you'll never get
there if you don't start.

This journal will guide you along the
way to be more productive, grateful,
confident, and inspired.

Celebrate your first small win... buying
this book. You are onto something great!

WEEK 1

Building good habits

This week, start with something simple, but important. Healthy habits lay the foundation for a more mindful, energized, and meaningful week.

WHAT IS ONE THING YOU WANT TO START DOING FOR YOURSELF TODAY?

A few ideas to get you started...
- *drink water in the morning*
- *wake up earlier*
- *say a prayer before bed*
- *go to sleep earlier*
- *clean and tidy up*
- *eat more fruits and vegetables*
- *walk more*
- *eat a healthy breakfast*

Building good habits

Now put that vision into action. Commit to doing that one thing you want to do at least **3 times** this week! Mark your progress below.

This week I commit to ...

_____

_____

Mark an X next to each time you complete your goal this week

ENTRY 01   **DATE**   /   /

☐   I did it! That was easy ...

ENTRY 02   **DATE**   /   /

☐   I did it! On to the next one ...

ENTRY 03   **DATE**   /   /

☐   I did it! I'm awesome!

WEEK 2

Mindset of gratitude

Great habits are only one part...gratitude and appreciation for yourself and others makes a world of difference. Keep up your habit this week, and each day, follow the prompts to get a little more appreciation in your life this week.

"A grateful heart is a magnet for miracles"

UNKNOWN

Mindset of gratitude

Each day this week, answer the prompts to practice gratitude and appreciation.

DAY 01   **DATE**   /   /

Today, I am grateful for...

_____

_____

_____

DAY 02   **DATE**   /   /

3 things that make me smile

1. _____

2. _____

3. _____

DAY 03   **DATE**   /   /

Today, I am grateful for...

_____

_____

_____

DAY 04   **DATE**   /   /

3 things that make me smile

1. _____

2. _____

3. _____

DAY 05   **DATE**   /   /

Today, I am grateful for...

_____

_____

_____

DAY 06   **DATE**   /   /

3 things that make me smile

1. _____

2. _____

3. _____

DAY 07   **DATE**   /   /

Today, I am grateful for...

_____

_____

WEEK 3

Encouraging affirmation

A grateful heart loves those around them as well as themselves. Affirmation reminds us to look inward and be thankful for our own gifts and talents. Affirmations are positive reminders or statements that can be used to encourage and motivate yourself or others. Often it's a lot easier to affirm others than it is ourselves, but we need to remember to encourage ourselves as well.

"I am worth celebrating myself"

Encouraging Affirmation

Each day this week, answer the prompts to practice self-love and affirmation

DAY 01   **DATE**   /   /
....

I am good at...

_____

_____

_____

DAY 02   **DATE**   /   /
....

3 things I love about myself

1. _____

2. _____

3. _____

DAY 03   **DATE**   /   /
....

Write down 1 career related affirmation and repeat it to yourself today

_____

_____

_____

DAY 04   **DATE**   **/**   **/**

Re write three negative thoughts with positive affirmation...
e.g. I am not alone; I am ready for love

1. _____

2. _____

3. _____

DAY 05   **DATE**   **/**   **/**

I am...

_____

_____

DAY 06   **DATE**   **/**   **/**

Write down 3 affirmations and repeat them to yourself today

1. _____

2. _____

3. _____

DAY 07   **DATE**   **/**   **/**

Today, I am thankful for my...

_____

_____

WEEK 4

Staying Inspired

The opposite of progress, is complacency. To move forward, we have to stretch beyond our comfort zones and get inspired. This week do something out of the norm that will bring a smile to your face.

A few ideas to get you started...

- *email an old friend*
- *treat yourself to ice cream at a ice cream shop*
- *buy yourself flowers*
- *buy something for a person in line behind you*
- *send a friend a card*

- *print out a picture from your phone*
- *Post something no one knows about you on social media*
- *make something with your hands*
- *do something you haven't done since you were a kid*
- *try a food you've never had before*

Don't live the same year 75 times and call it a life."

ROBIN SHARMA

Staying Inspired

Each day this week, choose an activity from the options provided or come up with your own way to get out of your comfort zone and stay inspired

DAY 01   **DATE**   /   /
· ·
Today I will...

_____

_____

DAY 02   **DATE**   /   /
· ·
Today I will...

_____

_____

DAY 03   **DATE**   /   /
· ·
Today I will...

_____

_____

DAY 04   **DATE**   /   /

Today I will...

_____

_____

DAY 05   **DATE**   /   /

Today I will...

_____

_____

DAY 06   **DATE**   /   /

Today I will...

_____

_____

DAY 07   **DATE**   /   /

Today I will...

_____

_____

Reflection

Overall, how do you feel?

terrible   not great   okay   good   fantastic!

My biggest "a ha" ...

_____

_____

_____

_____

_____

_____

_____

The most challenging activity for me ...? Why?

_____

_____

_____

_____

_____

_____

_____

_____

WEEK 5
Building good habits

This week, continue to build on the great progress and momentum you've had. Step it up this week with another healthy habit.

This week I commit to ...

_____

_____

ENTRY 01   **DATE**   /   /
....

☐   I did it! That was easy ...

ENTRY 02   **DATE**   /   /
....

☐   I did it! On to the next one ...

ENTRY 03   **DATE**   /   /
....

☐   I did it! Wahoo!

───────────────◁◆▷───────────────

A few ideas to get you started...
- *drink water in the morning*
- *wake up earlier*
- *say a prayer before bed*
- *go to sleep earlier*
- *clean and tidy up*
- *eat more fruits and vegetables*
- *walk more*
- *eat a healthy breakfast*

WEEK 6
Mindset of gratitude

DAY 01   **DATE**   /   /

Today, I am grateful for...

_____

_____

DAY 02   **DATE**   /   /

3 things that make me smile

1. _____

2. _____

3. _____

DAY 03   **DATE**   /   /

Today, I am grateful for...

_____

_____

DAY 04   **DATE**   /   /

3 things that make me smile

1. _____

2. _____

3. _____

DAY 05   **DATE**   /   /

Today, I am grateful for...

_____

_____

DAY 06   **DATE**   /   /

3 things that make me smile

1. _____

2. _____

3. _____

DAY 07   **DATE**   /   /

Today, I am grateful for...

_____

_____

WEEK 7
Encouraging Affirmation

DAY 01 **DATE** / /

I am good at...

_____

_____

DAY 02 **DATE** / /

3 things I love about myself

1. _____

2. _____

3. _____

DAY 03 **DATE** / /

Write down 1 career related affirmation and repeat it to yourself today

_____

_____

DAY 04   **DATE**   /   /

Re write three negative thoughts with positive affirmation...
e.g. I am not alone; I am ready for love

1. _____

2. _____

3. _____

DAY 05   **DATE**   /   /

I am...

_____

_____

_____

DAY 06   **DATE**   /   /

Write down 3 affirmations and repeat them to yourself today

1. _____

2. _____

3. _____

DAY 07   **DATE**   /   /

Today, I am thankful for my...

_____

_____

WEEK 8
Staying Inspired

DAY 01　　　　**DATE**　　/　　/
· ·
Today I will...

_____

_____

DAY 02　　　　**DATE**　　/　　/
· ·
Today I will...

_____

_____

DAY 03　　　　**DATE**　　/　　/
· ·
Today I will...

_____

_____

A few ideas to get you started...

- email an old friend
- buy yourself flowers
- buy something for a person in line behind you
- send a friend a card
- print out a funny picture from your phone
- make something with your hands
- do something you haven't done since you were a kid
- try a food you've never had before

DAY 04   **DATE**   /   /

Today I will...

_____

_____

DAY 05   **DATE**   /   /

Today I will...

_____

_____

DAY 06   **DATE**   /   /

Today I will...

_____

_____

DAY 07   **DATE**   /   /

Today I will...

_____

_____

Reflection

Overall, how do you feel?

terrible   not great   okay   good   fantastic!

My highlight so far has been...

_____

_____

_____

_____

_____

_____

_____

_____

What are you learning about yourself?

_____

_____

_____

_____

_____

_____

_____

_____

WEEK 9
Building good habits

This week I commit to ...

_____

_____

ENTRY 01   **DATE**   /   /
· ·

☐   I did it! That was easy ...

ENTRY 02   **DATE**   /   /
· ·

☐   I did it! On to the next one ...

ENTRY 03   **DATE**   /   /
· ·

☐   I did it! Wahoo!

───────────────────◄◆►───────────────────

A few ideas to get you started...

- *drink water in the morning*
- *wake up earlier*
- *say a prayer before bed*
- *go to sleep earlier*

- *clean and tidy up*
- *eat more fruits and vegetables*
- *walk more*
- *eat a healthy breakfast*

WEEK 10
Mindset of gratitude

DAY 01   **DATE**   /   /
....

Today, I am grateful for...

_____

_____

DAY 02   **DATE**   /   /
....

3 things that make me smile

1. _____

2. _____

3. _____

DAY 03   **DATE**   /   /
....

Today, I am grateful for...

_____

_____

DAY 04   **DATE**   /   /

3 things that make me smile

1. _____

2. _____

3. _____

DAY 05   **DATE**   /   /

Today, I am grateful for...

_____

_____

DAY 06   **DATE**   /   /

3 things that make me smile

1. _____

2. _____

3. _____

DAY 07   **DATE**   /   /

Today, I am grateful for...

_____

_____

WEEK 11
Encouraging Affirmation

DAY 01 **DATE** / /

I am good at...

_____

_____

DAY 02 **DATE** / /

3 things I love about myself

1. _____

2. _____

3. _____

DAY 03 **DATE** / /

Write down 1 career related affirmation and repeat it to yourself today

_____

_____

DAY 04   **DATE**   /   /

Re write three negative thoughts with positive affirmation...
e.g. I am not alone; I am ready for love

1. _____

2. _____

3. _____

DAY 05   **DATE**   /   /

I am...

_____

_____

_____

DAY 06   **DATE**   /   /

Write down 3 affirmations and repeat them to yourself today

1. _____

2. _____

3. _____

DAY 07   **DATE**   /   /

Today, I am thankful for my...

_____

_____

WEEK 12
Staying Inspired

DAY 01　　　　　　**DATE**　　　/　　　　/

· ·

Today I will...

_____

_____

DAY 02　　　　　　**DATE**　　　/　　　　/

· ·

Today I will...

_____

_____

DAY 03　　　　　　**DATE**　　　/　　　　/

· ·

Today I will...

_____

_____

A few ideas to get you started...

- *email an old friend*
- *buy yourself flowers*
- *buy something for a person in line behind you*
- *send a friend a card*

- *print out a funny picture from your phone*
- *make something with your hands*
- *do something you haven't done since you were a kid*
- *try a food you've never had before*

DAY 04   **DATE**   /   /

Today I will...

_____

_____

DAY 05   **DATE**   /   /

Today I will...

_____

_____

DAY 06   **DATE**   /   /

Today I will...

_____

_____

DAY 07   **DATE**   /   /

Today I will...

_____

_____

Reflection

Overall, how do you feel?

terrible   not great   okay   good   fantastic!

Look back at previous entries, and write about what
has changed the most for you

_____

_____

_____

_____

_____

_____

_____

_____

_____

_____

_____

_____

_____

_____

_____

_____

WEEK 13
Building good habits

This week, continue to build on the great progress and momentum you've had. Step it up this week with another healthy habit.

This week I commit to ...

_____

_____

ENTRY 01   **DATE**   /   /

☐   I did it! That was easy ...

ENTRY 02   **DATE**   /   /

☐   I did it! On to the next one ...

ENTRY 03   **DATE**   /   /

☐   I did it! Wahoo!

A few ideas to get you started...

- *drink water in the morning*
- *wake up earlier*
- *say a prayer before bed*
- *go to sleep earlier*
- *clean and tidy up*
- *eat more fruits and vegetables*
- *walk more*
- *eat a healthy breakfast*

WEEK 14
Mindset of gratitude

DAY 01　　　　　　**DATE**　　／　　／

Today, I am grateful for...

_____

_____

DAY 02　　　　　　**DATE**　　／　　／

3 things that make me smile

1. _____

2. _____

3. _____

DAY 03　　　　　　**DATE**　　／　　／

Today, I am grateful for...

_____

_____

DAY 04   **DATE**   /   /

3 things that make me smile

1. _____

2. _____

3. _____

DAY 05   **DATE**   /   /

Today, I am grateful for...

_____

_____

DAY 06   **DATE**   /   /

3 things that make me smile

1. _____

2. _____

3. _____

DAY 07   **DATE**   /   /

Today, I am grateful for...

_____

_____

WEEK 15
Encouraging Affirmation

DAY 01　　　　**DATE**　　/　　/

I am good at...

_____

_____

DAY 02　　　　**DATE**　　/　　/

3 things I love about myself

1. _____

2. _____

3. _____

DAY 03　　　　**DATE**　　/　　/

Write down 1 career related affirmation and repeat it to yourself today

_____

_____

DAY 04   **DATE**   /   /
••
Re write three negative thoughts with positive affirmation...
e.g. I am not alone; I am ready for love

1. _____

2. _____

3. _____

DAY 05   **DATE**   /   /
••
I am...

_____

_____

_____

DAY 06   **DATE**   /   /
••
Write down 3 affirmations and repeat them to yourself today

1. _____

2. _____

3. _____

DAY 07   **DATE**   /   /
••
Today, I am thankful for my...

_____

_____

WEEK 16
Staying Inspired

DAY 01   **DATE**   /   /

Today I will...

_____

_____

DAY 02   **DATE**   /   /

Today I will...

_____

_____

DAY 03   **DATE**   /   /

Today I will...

_____

_____

A few ideas to get you started...

- *email an old friend*
- *buy yourself flowers*
- *buy something for a person in line behind you*
- *send a friend a card*

- *print out a funny picture from your phone*
- *make something with your hands*
- *do something you haven't done since you were a kid*
- *try a food you've never had before*

DAY 04 **DATE**   /   /

· ·

Today I will...

_____

_____

DAY 05 **DATE**   /   /

· ·

Today I will...

_____

_____

DAY 06 **DATE**   /   /

· ·

Today I will...

_____

_____

DAY 07 **DATE**   /   /

· ·

Today I will...

_____

_____

Reflection

Overall, how do you feel?

terrible   not great   okay   good   fantastic!

The affirmation that spoke to me the most was...

_____

_____

_____

_____

_____

_____

_____

_____

I am looking forward to...

_____

_____

_____

_____

_____

_____

_____

_____

WEEK 17
Building good habits

> *"You are never too old to set another goal or to dream a new dream."*
>
> C.S. LEWIS

This week I commit to ...

_____

_____

ENTRY 01   **DATE**   /   /
....

☐   I did it! That was easy ...

ENTRY 02   **DATE**   /   /
....

☐   I did it! On to the next one ...

ENTRY 03   **DATE**   /   /
....

☐   I did it! Wahoo!

A few ideas to get you started...
- *drink water in the morning*
- *wake up earlier*
- *say a prayer before bed*
- *go to sleep earlier*

- *clean and tidy up*
- *eat more fruits and vegetables*
- *walk more*
- *eat a healthy breakfast*

WEEK 18
Mindset of gratitude

DAY 01 DATE / /

Today, I am grateful for...

_____

_____

DAY 02 DATE / /

3 things that make me smile

1. _____

2. _____

3. _____

DAY 03 DATE / /

Today, I am grateful for...

_____

_____

DAY 04　　　　　　**DATE**　　　/　　　　/

· ·

3 things that make me smile

1. _____

2. _____

3. _____

DAY 05　　　　　　**DATE**　　　/　　　　/

· ·

Today, I am grateful for...

_____

_____

DAY 06　　　　　　**DATE**　　　/　　　　/

· ·

3 things that make me smile

1. _____

2. _____

3. _____

DAY 07　　　　　　**DATE**　　　/　　　　/

· ·

Today, I am grateful for...

_____

_____

WEEK 19
Encouraging Affirmation

DAY 01 **DATE** / /

I am good at...

_____

_____

DAY 02 **DATE** / /

3 things I love about myself

1. _____

2. _____

3. _____

DAY 03 **DATE** / /

Write down 1 career related affirmation and repeat it to yourself today

_____

_____

DAY 04   **DATE** / /

Re write three negative thoughts with positive affirmation...
e.g. I am not alone; I am ready for love

1. _____

2. _____

3. _____

DAY 05   **DATE** / /

I am...

_____

_____

_____

DAY 06   **DATE** / /

Write down 3 affirmations and repeat them to yourself today

1. _____

2. _____

3. _____

DAY 07   **DATE** / /

Today, I am thankful for my...

_____

_____

WEEK 20
Staying Inspired

DAY 01　　　　**DATE**　　/　　/

Today I will...

_____

_____

DAY 02　　　　**DATE**　　/　　/

Today I will...

_____

_____

DAY 03　　　　**DATE**　　/　　/

Today I will...

_____

_____

A few ideas to get you started...

- *email an old friend*
- *buy yourself flowers*
- *buy something for a person in line behind you*
- *send a friend a card*

- *print out a funny picture from your phone*
- *make something with your hands*
- *do something you haven't done since you were a kid*
- *try a food you've never had before*

DAY 04   **DATE**   /   /

Today I will...

_____

_____

DAY 05   **DATE**   /   /

Today I will...

_____

_____

DAY 06   **DATE**   /   /

Today I will...

_____

_____

DAY 07   **DATE**   /   /

Today I will...

_____

_____

Reflection

Overall, how do you feel?

terrible   not great   okay   good   fantastic!

My biggest "a ha" ...

_____

_____

_____

_____

_____

_____

_____

_____

I want to remember to be especially grateful for...

_____

_____

_____

_____

_____

_____

_____

_____

WEEK 21
Building good habits

This week I commit to ...

_____

_____

ENTRY 01   **DATE**   /   /

· ·

☐   I did it! That was easy ...

ENTRY 02   **DATE**   /   /

· ·

☐   I did it! On to the next one ...

ENTRY 03   **DATE**   /   /

· ·

☐   I did it! Wahoo!

───────────────◁◆▷───────────────

A few ideas to get you started...
- *drink water in the morning*
- *wake up earlier*
- *say a prayer before bed*
- *go to sleep earlier*

- *clean and tidy up*
- *eat more fruits and vegetables*
- *walk more*
- *eat a healthy breakfast*

WEEK 22
Mindset of gratitude

DAY 01   **DATE**   /   /

Today, I am grateful for...

_____

_____

DAY 02   **DATE**   /   /

3 things that make me smile

1. _____

2. _____

3. _____

DAY 03   **DATE**   /   /

Today, I am grateful for...

_____

_____

DAY 04 **DATE** / /

3 things that make me smile

1. _____

2. _____

3. _____

DAY 05 **DATE** / /

Today, I am grateful for...

_____

_____

DAY 06 **DATE** / /

3 things that make me smile

1. _____

2. _____

3. _____

DAY 07 **DATE** / /

Today, I am grateful for...

_____

_____

WEEK 23
Encouraging Affirmation

DAY 01   **DATE**   /   /

I am good at...

_____

_____

DAY 02   **DATE**   /   /

3 things I love about myself

1. _____

2. _____

3. _____

DAY 03   **DATE**   /   /

Write down 1 career related affirmation and repeat it to yourself today

_____

_____

DAY 04 **DATE** / /

Re write three negative thoughts with positive affirmation...
e.g. I am not alone; I am ready for love

1. _____

2. _____

3. _____

DAY 05 **DATE** / /

I am...

_____

_____

_____

DAY 06 **DATE** / /

Write down 3 affirmations and repeat them to yourself today

1. _____

2. _____

3. _____

DAY 07 **DATE** / /

Today, I am thankful for my...

_____

_____

WEEK 24
Staying Inspired

DAY 01   **DATE**   /   /

Today I will...

_____

_____

DAY 02   **DATE**   /   /

Today I will...

_____

_____

DAY 03   **DATE**   /   /

Today I will...

_____

_____

A few ideas to get you started...

- email an old friend
- buy yourself flowers
- buy something for a person in line behind you
- send a friend a card

- print out a funny picture from your phone
- make something with your hands
- do something you haven't done since you were a kid
- try a food you've never had before

DAY 04   **DATE**   /   /

Today I will...

_____

_____

DAY 05   **DATE**   /   /

Today I will...

_____

_____

DAY 06   **DATE**   /   /

Today I will...

_____

_____

DAY 07   **DATE**   /   /

Today I will...

_____

_____

Reflection

Overall, how do you feel?

terrible   not great   okay   good   fantastic!

I was most surprised by...

_____

_____

_____

_____

_____

_____

_____

_____

My life is great because...

_____

_____

_____

_____

_____

_____

_____

_____

WEEK 25
Building good habits

This week, continue to build on the great progress and momentum you've had. Step it up this week with another healthy habit.

This week I commit to ...

_____

_____

ENTRY 01   **DATE**   /   /
....

☐   I did it! That was easy ...

ENTRY 02   **DATE**   /   /
....

☐   I did it! On to the next one ...

ENTRY 03   **DATE**   /   /
....

☐   I did it! Wahoo!

◀◆▷

A few ideas to get you started...
- *drink water in the morning*
- *wake up earlier*
- *say a prayer before bed*
- *go to sleep earlier*
- *clean and tidy up*
- *eat more fruits and vegetables*
- *walk more*
- *eat a healthy breakfast*

WEEK 26
Mindset of gratitude

DAY 01   **DATE**   /   /

Today, I am grateful for...

_____

_____

DAY 02   **DATE**   /   /

3 things that make me smile

1. _____

2. _____

3. _____

DAY 03   **DATE**   /   /

Today, I am grateful for...

_____

_____

DAY 04   **DATE**   /   /

3 things that make me smile

1. _____

2. _____

3. _____

DAY 05   **DATE**   /   /

Today, I am grateful for...

_____

_____

DAY 06   **DATE**   /   /

3 things that make me smile

1. _____

2. _____

3. _____

DAY 07   **DATE**   /   /

Today, I am grateful for...

_____

_____

WEEK 27
Encouraging Affirmation

DAY 01   **DATE**   /   /

I am good at...

_____

_____

DAY 02   **DATE**   /   /

3 things I love about myself

1. _____

2. _____

3. _____

DAY 03   **DATE**   /   /

Write down 1 career related affirmation and repeat it to yourself today

_____

_____

DAY 04 DATE / /

Re write three negative thoughts with positive affirmation...
e.g. I am not alone; I am ready for love

1. _____

2. _____

3. _____

DAY 05 DATE / /

I am...

_____

_____

_____

DAY 06 DATE / /

Write down 3 affirmations and repeat them to yourself today

1. _____

2. _____

3. _____

DAY 07 DATE / /

Today, I am thankful for my...

_____

_____

WEEK 28
Staying Inspired

DAY 01   **DATE**   /   /

Today I will...

_____

_____

DAY 02   **DATE**   /   /

Today I will...

_____

_____

DAY 03   **DATE**   /   /

Today I will...

_____

_____

A few ideas to get you started...

- *email an old friend*
- *buy yourself flowers*
- *buy something for a person in line behind you*
- *send a friend a card*

- *print out a funny picture from your phone*
- *make something with your hands*
- *do something you haven't done since you were a kid*
- *try a food you've never had before*

DAY 04   **DATE**   /   /

Today I will...

_____

_____

DAY 05   **DATE**   /   /

Today I will...

_____

_____

DAY 06   **DATE**   /   /

Today I will...

_____

_____

DAY 07   **DATE**   /   /

Today I will...

_____

_____

Reflection

Overall, how do you feel?

terrible   not great   okay   good   fantastic!

My biggest "a ha" ...

_____

_____

_____

_____

_____

_____

_____

_____

What in my life is a barrier to living with intention?

_____

_____

_____

_____

_____

_____

_____

_____

_____

WEEK 29
Building
good habits

This week I commit to ...

_____

_____

ENTRY 01   **DATE**   /   /
....

☐   I did it! That was easy ...

ENTRY 02   **DATE**   /   /
....

☐   I did it! On to the next one ...

ENTRY 03   **DATE**   /   /
....

☐   I did it! Wahoo!

◁◆▷

A few ideas to get you started...
- *drink water in the morning*
- *wake up earlier*
- *say a prayer before bed*
- *go to sleep earlier*

- *clean and tidy up*
- *eat more fruits and vegetables*
- *walk more*
- *eat a healthy breakfast*

WEEK 30
Mindset of gratitude

DAY 01   **DATE**   /   /

Today, I am grateful for...

_____

_____

DAY 02   **DATE**   /   /

3 things that make me smile

1. _____

2. _____

3. _____

DAY 03   **DATE**   /   /

Today, I am grateful for...

_____

_____

DAY 04   **DATE**   /   /

3 things that make me smile

1. _____

2. _____

3. _____

DAY 05   **DATE**   /   /

Today, I am grateful for...

_____

_____

DAY 06   **DATE**   /   /

3 things that make me smile

1. _____

2. _____

3. _____

DAY 07   **DATE**   /   /

Today, I am grateful for...

_____

_____

WEEK 31
Encouraging Affirmation

> *"You are enough just as you are."*
>
> MEGHAN MARKLE

DAY 01   **DATE**   /   /
....

I am good at...

_____

_____

DAY 02   **DATE**   /   /
....

3 things I love about myself

1. _____

2. _____

3. _____

DAY 03   **DATE**   /   /
....

Write down 1 career related affirmation and repeat it to yourself today

_____

_____

DAY 04   **DATE**   /   /

Re write three negative thoughts with positive affirmation...
e.g. I am not alone; I am ready for love

1. _____

2. _____

3. _____

DAY 05   **DATE**   /   /

I am...

_____

_____

_____

DAY 06   **DATE**   /   /

Write down 3 affirmations and repeat them to yourself today

1. _____

2. _____

3. _____

DAY 07   **DATE**   /   /

Today, I am thankful for my...

_____

_____

WEEK 32
Staying Inspired

DAY 01 **DATE** / /

Today I will...

_____

_____

DAY 02 **DATE** / /

Today I will...

_____

_____

DAY 03 **DATE** / /

Today I will...

_____

_____

A few ideas to get you started...

- email an old friend
- buy yourself flowers
- buy something for a person in line behind you
- send a friend a card
- print out a funny picture from your phone
- make something with your hands
- do something you haven't done since you were a kid
- try a food you've never had before

DAY 04   **DATE**   /   /

· ·

Today I will...

_____

_____

DAY 05   **DATE**   /   /

· ·

Today I will...

_____

_____

DAY 06   **DATE**   /   /

· ·

Today I will...

_____

_____

DAY 07   **DATE**   /   /

· ·

Today I will...

_____

_____

Reflection

Overall, how do you feel?

terrible   not great   okay   good   fantastic!

Write a letter to your future self. Explain how proud you are of what you've accomplished and what is to come.

_____

_____

_____

_____

_____

_____

_____

_____

_____

_____

_____

_____

_____

_____

_____

_____

WEEK 33
Building good habits

This week I commit to ...

_____

_____

ENTRY 01   **DATE**   /   /
....

☐   I did it! That was easy ...

ENTRY 02   **DATE**   /   /
....

☐   I did it! On to the next one ...

ENTRY 03   **DATE**   /   /
....

☐   I did it! Wahoo!

A few ideas to get you started...
- *drink water in the morning*
- *wake up earlier*
- *say a prayer before bed*
- *go to sleep earlier*

- *clean and tidy up*
- *eat more fruits and vegetables*
- *walk more*
- *eat a healthy breakfast*

WEEK 34
Mindset of gratitude

DAY 01   **DATE**   /   /

Today, I am grateful for...

_____

_____

DAY 02   **DATE**   /   /

3 things that make me smile

1. _____

2. _____

3. _____

DAY 03   **DATE**   /   /

Today, I am grateful for...

_____

_____

DAY 04   **DATE**   /   /

3 things that make me smile

1. _____

2. _____

3. _____

DAY 05   **DATE**   /   /

Today, I am grateful for...

_____

_____

DAY 06   **DATE**   /   /

3 things that make me smile

1. _____

2. _____

3. _____

DAY 07   **DATE**   /   /

Today, I am grateful for...

_____

_____

WEEK 35
Encouraging Affirmation

"If you have good thoughts they will shine out of your face like sunbeams and you will always look lovely."

ROALD DAHL

DAY 01   **DATE**   /   /

I am good at...

_____

_____

DAY 02   **DATE**   /   /

3 things I love about myself

1. _____

2. _____

3. _____

DAY 03   **DATE**   /   /

Write down 1 career related affirmation and repeat it to yourself today

_____

_____

DAY 04   **DATE**   /   /

Re write three negative thoughts with positive affirmation...
e.g. I am not alone; I am ready for love

1. _____

2. _____

3. _____

DAY 05   **DATE**   /   /

I am...

_____

_____

_____

DAY 06   **DATE**   /   /

Write down 3 affirmations and repeat them to yourself today

1. _____

2. _____

3. _____

DAY 07   **DATE**   /   /

Today, I am thankful for my...

_____

_____

WEEK 36
Staying Inspired

DAY 01   **DATE**   /   /

Today I will...

_____

_____

DAY 02   **DATE**   /   /

Today I will...

_____

_____

DAY 03   **DATE**   /   /

Today I will...

_____

_____

A few ideas to get you started...

- email an old friend
- buy yourself flowers
- buy something for a person in line behind you
- send a friend a card
- print out a funny picture from your phone
- make something with your hands
- do something you haven't done since you were a kid
- try a food you've never had before

DAY 04   **DATE**   /   /

Today I will...

_____

_____

DAY 05   **DATE**   /   /

Today I will...

_____

_____

DAY 06   **DATE**   /   /

Today I will...

_____

_____

DAY 07   **DATE**   /   /

Today I will...

_____

_____

Reflection

Overall, how do you feel?

terrible   not great   okay   good   fantastic!

For the first time I ... and it felt...

_____

_____

_____

_____

_____

_____

_____

The most challenging activity for me ...? Why?

_____

_____

_____

_____

_____

_____

_____

_____

WEEK 37
Building good habits

This week I commit to ...

_____

_____

ENTRY 01   **DATE**   /   /
....

☐   I did it! That was easy ...

ENTRY 02   **DATE**   /   /
....

☐   I did it! On to the next one ...

ENTRY 03   **DATE**   /   /
....

☐   I did it! Wahoo!

◀◆▷

A few ideas to get you started...
- *drink water in the morning*
- *wake up earlier*
- *say a prayer before bed*
- *go to sleep earlier*
- *clean and tidy up*
- *eat more fruits and vegetables*
- *walk more*
- *eat a healthy breakfast*

WEEK 38
Mindset of gratitude

DAY 01   **DATE**   /   /

Today, I am grateful for...

_____

_____

DAY 02   **DATE**   /   /

3 things that make me smile

1. _____

2. _____

3. _____

DAY 03   **DATE**   /   /

Today, I am grateful for...

_____

_____

DAY 04   **DATE**   /   /

3 things that make me smile

1. _____

2. _____

3. _____

DAY 05   **DATE**   /   /

Today, I am grateful for...

_____

_____

DAY 06   **DATE**   /   /

3 things that make me smile

1. _____

2. _____

3. _____

DAY 07   **DATE**   /   /

Today, I am grateful for...

_____

_____

WEEK 39
Encouraging Affirmation

> *"Be gentle with yourself, learn to love yourself, to forgive yourself, for only as we have the right attitude toward ourselves can we have the right attitude toward others."*
>
> WILFRED PETERSON

DAY 01   **DATE**   /   /

I am good at...

_____

_____

DAY 02   **DATE**   /   /

3 things I love about myself

1. _____

2. _____

3. _____

DAY 03   **DATE**   /   /

Write down 1 career related affirmation and repeat it to yourself today

_____

_____

DAY 04 DATE   /   /
....

Re write three negative thoughts with positive affirmation...
e.g. I am not alone; I am ready for love

1. _____

2. _____

3. _____

DAY 05 DATE   /   /
....

I am...

_____

_____

_____

DAY 06 DATE   /   /
....

Write down 3 affirmations and repeat them to yourself today

1. _____

2. _____

3. _____

DAY 07 DATE   /   /
....

Today, I am thankful for my...

_____

_____

WEEK 40
Staying Inspired

DAY 01 **DATE** / /

Today I will...

_____

_____

DAY 02 **DATE** / /

Today I will...

_____

_____

DAY 03 **DATE** / /

Today I will...

_____

_____

A few ideas to get you started...

- *email an old friend*
- *buy yourself flowers*
- *buy something for a person in line behind you*
- *send a friend a card*

- *print out a funny picture from your phone*
- *make something with your hands*
- *do something you haven't done since you were a kid*
- *try a food you've never had before*

DAY 04 DATE / /

· ·

Today I will...

_____

_____

DAY 05 DATE / /

· ·

Today I will...

_____

_____

DAY 06 DATE / /

· ·

Today I will...

_____

_____

DAY 07 DATE / /

· ·

Today I will...

_____

_____

Reflection

Overall, how do you feel?

terrible   not great   okay   good   fantastic!

My happiest moment was...

_____

_____

_____

_____

_____

_____

_____

I am looking forward to...

_____

_____

_____

_____

_____

_____

_____

_____

WEEK 41
Building
good habits

This week I commit to ...

_____

_____

ENTRY 01   **DATE**   /   /
....

☐   I did it! That was easy ...

ENTRY 02   **DATE**   /   /
....

☐   I did it! On to the next one ...

ENTRY 03   **DATE**   /   /
....

☐   I did it! Wahoo!

A few ideas to get you started...
- *drink water in the morning*
- *wake up earlier*
- *say a prayer before bed*
- *go to sleep earlier*
- *clean and tidy up*
- *eat more fruits and vegetables*
- *walk more*
- *eat a healthy breakfast*

WEEK 42
Mindset of gratitude

DAY 01 **DATE**   /   /

Today, I am grateful for...

_____

_____

DAY 02 **DATE**   /   /

3 things that make me smile

1. _____

2. _____

3. _____

DAY 03 **DATE**   /   /

Today, I am grateful for...

_____

_____

DAY 04   **DATE**   /   /

3 things that make me smile

1. _____

2. _____

3. _____

DAY 05   **DATE**   /   /

Today, I am grateful for...

_____

_____

DAY 06   **DATE**   /   /

3 things that make me smile

1. _____

2. _____

3. _____

DAY 07   **DATE**   /   /

Today, I am grateful for...

_____

_____

WEEK 43
Encouraging Affirmation

"I don't like myself, I'm crazy about myself."

MAY WEST

DAY 01   **DATE**   /   /

I am good at...

_____

_____

DAY 02   **DATE**   /   /

3 things I love about myself

1. _____

2. _____

3. _____

DAY 03   **DATE**   /   /

Write down 1 career related affirmation and repeat it to yourself today

_____

_____

DAY 04   **DATE**   /   /

Re write three negative thoughts with positive affirmation...
e.g. I am not alone; I am ready for love

1. _____

2. _____

3. _____

DAY 05   **DATE**   /   /

I am...

_____

_____

_____

DAY 06   **DATE**   /   /

Write down 3 affirmations and repeat them to yourself today

1. _____

2. _____

3. _____

DAY 07   **DATE**   /   /

Today, I am thankful for my...

_____

_____

WEEK 44
Staying Inspired

DAY 01   **DATE**   /   /

• •

Today I will...

_____

_____

DAY 02   **DATE**   /   /

• •

Today I will...

_____

_____

DAY 03   **DATE**   /   /

• •

Today I will...

_____

_____

A few ideas to get you started...

- *email an old friend*
- *buy yourself flowers*
- *buy something for a person in line behind you*
- *send a friend a card*
- *print out a funny picture from your phone*
- *make something with your hands*
- *do something you haven't done since you were a kid*
- *try a food you've never had before*

DAY 04   **DATE**   /   /

Today I will...

_____

_____

DAY 05   **DATE**   /   /

Today I will...

_____

_____

DAY 06   **DATE**   /   /

Today I will...

_____

_____

DAY 07   **DATE**   /   /

Today I will...

_____

_____

Reflection

Overall, how do you feel?

terrible   not great   okay   good   fantastic!

My biggest "a ha" ...

_____

_____

_____

_____

_____

_____

I learned ...

_____

_____

_____

_____

_____

_____

_____

_____

WEEK 45
Building good habits

This week I commit to ...

_____

_____

ENTRY 01　　　　　**DATE**　　/　　　/

☐　I did it! That was easy ...

ENTRY 02　　　　　**DATE**　　/　　　/

☐　I did it! On to the next one ...

ENTRY 03　　　　　**DATE**　　/　　　/

☐　I did it! Wahoo!

A few ideas to get you started...
- *drink water in the morning*
- *wake up earlier*
- *say a prayer before bed*
- *go to sleep earlier*

- *clean and tidy up*
- *eat more fruits and vegetables*
- *walk more*
- *eat a healthy breakfast*

WEEK 46
Mindset of gratitude

DAY 01   **DATE**   /   /

Today, I am grateful for...

_____

_____

DAY 02   **DATE**   /   /

3 things that make me smile

1. _____

2. _____

3. _____

DAY 03   **DATE**   /   /

Today, I am grateful for...

_____

_____

DAY 04   **DATE**   /   /

3 things that make me smile

1. _____
2. _____
3. _____

DAY 05   **DATE**   /   /

Today, I am grateful for...

_____

_____

DAY 06   **DATE**   /   /

3 things that make me smile

1. _____
2. _____
3. _____

DAY 07   **DATE**   /   /

Today, I am grateful for...

_____

_____

WEEK 47
Encouraging Affirmation

> *"What lies behind us and what lies before us are tiny matters compared to what lies within us."*
>
> RALPH WALDO EMERSON

DAY 01   **DATE**   /   /

I am good at...

_____

_____

DAY 02   **DATE**   /   /

3 things I love about myself

1. _____

2. _____

3. _____

DAY 03   **DATE**   /   /

Write down 1 career related affirmation and repeat it to yourself today

_____

_____

DAY 04   **DATE**   /   /

Re write three negative thoughts with positive affirmation...
e.g. I am not alone; I am ready for love

1. _____

2. _____

3. _____

DAY 05   **DATE**   /   /

I am...

_____

_____

_____

DAY 06   **DATE**   /   /

Write down 3 affirmations and repeat them to yourself today

1. _____

2. _____

3. _____

DAY 07   **DATE**   /   /

Today, I am thankful for my...

_____

_____

WEEK 48
Staying Inspired

DAY 01 **DATE** / /

Today I will...

_____

_____

DAY 02 **DATE** / /

Today I will...

_____

_____

DAY 03 **DATE** / /

Today I will...

_____

_____

A few ideas to get you started...

- *email an old friend*
- *buy yourself flowers*
- *buy something for a person in line behind you*
- *send a friend a card*

- *print out a funny picture from your phone*
- *make something with your hands*
- *do something you haven't done since you were a kid*
- *try a food you've never had before*

DAY 04   **DATE**   /   /

Today I will...

_____

_____

DAY 05   **DATE**   /   /

Today I will...

_____

_____

DAY 06   **DATE**   /   /

Today I will...

_____

_____

DAY 07   **DATE**   /   /

Today I will...

_____

_____

Reflection

Overall, how do you feel?

terrible   not great   okay   good   fantastic!

My biggest "a ha" ...

_____

_____

_____

_____

_____

_____

_____

_____

The most challenging activity for me ...? Why?

_____

_____

_____

_____

_____

_____

_____

_____

WEEK 49
Building good habits

This week I commit to ...

_____

_____

ENTRY 01   **DATE**   /   /

☐   I did it! That was easy ...

ENTRY 02   **DATE**   /   /

☐   I did it! On to the next one ...

ENTRY 03   **DATE**   /   /

☐   I did it! Wahoo!

A few ideas to get you started...

- *drink water in the morning*
- *wake up earlier*
- *say a prayer before bed*
- *go to sleep earlier*
- *clean and tidy up*
- *eat more fruits and vegetables*
- *walk more*
- *eat a healthy breakfast*

WEEK 50
Mindset of gratitude

DAY 01   **DATE**   /   /

· ·

Today, I am grateful for...

_____

_____

DAY 02   **DATE**   /   /

· ·

3 things that make me smile

1. _____

2. _____

3. _____

DAY 03   **DATE**   /   /

· ·

Today, I am grateful for...

_____

_____

DAY 04   **DATE**   /   /

3 things that make me smile

1. _____

2. _____

3. _____

DAY 05   **DATE**   /   /

Today, I am grateful for...

_____

_____

DAY 06   **DATE**   /   /

3 things that make me smile

1. _____

2. _____

3. _____

DAY 07   **DATE**   /   /

Today, I am grateful for...

_____

_____

WEEK 51
Encouraging Affirmation

"To love yourself right now, just as you are, is to give yourself heaven."

ALAN COHEN

DAY 01   **DATE** /   /

I am good at...

_____

_____

DAY 02   **DATE** /   /

3 things I love about myself

1. _____

2. _____

3. _____

DAY 03   **DATE** /   /

Write down 1 career related affirmation and repeat it to yourself today

_____

_____

DAY 04   **DATE**   /   /

Re write three negative thoughts with positive affirmation...
e.g. I am not alone; I am ready for love

1. _____

2. _____

3. _____

DAY 05   **DATE**   /   /

I am...

_____

_____

_____

DAY 06   **DATE**   /   /

Write down 3 affirmations and repeat them to yourself today

1. _____

2. _____

3. _____

DAY 07   **DATE**   /   /

Today, I am thankful for my...

_____

_____

WEEK 52
Staying Inspired

DAY 01   **DATE**   /   /

Today I will...

_____

_____

DAY 02   **DATE**   /   /

Today I will...

_____

_____

DAY 03   **DATE**   /   /

Today I will...

_____

_____

A few ideas to get you started...

- email an old friend
- buy yourself flowers
- buy something for a person in line behind you
- send a friend a card

- print out a funny picture from your phone
- make something with your hands
- do something you haven't done since you were a kid
- try a food you've never had before

DAY 04   **DATE**   /   /

Today I will...

_____

_____

DAY 05   **DATE**   /   /

Today I will...

_____

_____

DAY 06   **DATE**   /   /

Today I will...

_____

_____

DAY 07   **DATE**   /   /

Today I will...

_____

_____

Reflection

Overall, how do you feel?

terrible not great okay good fantastic!

This journal has helped me...

_____

_____

_____

_____

_____

_____

I want to share this with...

_____

_____

_____

_____

_____

_____

_____

FINAL THOUGHTS

FINAL THOUGHTS

A year of intention

PAY IT FORWARD...

Made in the USA
Las Vegas, NV
02 August 2024